Original title:
The Heart's Hidden Hieroglyphs

Copyright © 2024 Creative Arts Management OÜ
All rights reserved.

Author: Harrison Blake
ISBN HARDBACK: 978-9916-90-770-2
ISBN PAPERBACK: 978-9916-90-771-9

Chronicles of the Unvoiced

In shadows deep, they softly tread,
Whispers lost, the words unsaid.
Silent tales within their eyes,
Echoes of the world's last sighs.

A canvas bare, the stories fade,
Crafted hearts in silence made.
With every glance, a truth unveiled,
In quiet storms, their strength prevailed.

Through alleys dark, they roam alone,
A melody in muted tone.
Each heartbeat thrums a secret call,
Together strong, they rise, not fall.

Beneath the stars, they shape their fate,
A tapestry of love and hate.
In the void, their spirits soar,
Unvoiced yet powerful at the core.

Guardians of Unexplored Feelings

In the silence, whispers grow,
Hidden dreams begin to flow.
Hearts bound tight, yet feel the space,
Unseen paths we dare to trace.

Echoes linger in the night,
Casting doubts in soft moonlight.
Each unspoken word we hold,
Guardians of stories untold.

Messages in Moonlight

Silver beams on quiet seas,
Gentle breezes weave through trees.
Secrets shared beneath the stars,
Weaving tales of who we are.

In shadows dance the dreams we hide,
Whispered truths we won't confide.
Moonlight carries every sigh,
Messages that never die.

Chiseled Shadows of Intimacy

In dusky corners, feelings bloom,
Chiseled edges carve the room.
Fingers brush like softest air,
Moments linger, hearts laid bare.

Captured glances, silent pleas,
Shadows waltz with gentle ease.
As daylight fades, we intertwine,
In the quiet, souls align.

Underneath the Skin's Script

Beneath the skin, a tale unfolds,
Deep within, where truth beholds.
Every scar, a mark of grace,
Whispers of the past we face.

In every heartbeat, stories trace,
Holding memories we embrace.
The language speaks in silent ways,
A script that time cannot erase.

Maps of Melancholy and Joy

In shadows cast by fading light,
Old pathways weave with fresh delight.
Each step we take, a story told,
In colors warm, in hues of gold.

Through valleys deep where whispers sigh,
The echoes fade, yet never die.
Mapping dreams on faded trails,
The heart prevails where silence wails.

Lines Inscribed in Moments Together

The clock ticks soft in the quiet night,
Two souls entwined, their laughter bright.
In every glance, a tale unfolds,
In whispered words, the heart consoles.

Beneath the stars, our worries cease,
In tender silence, we find our peace.
Each fleeting glance, a canvas bare,
Painted in love, beyond compare.

The Emblem of Remembered Caresses

Fingers trace where dreams reside,
In gentle warmth, our hearts collide.
A brush of skin, a shiver's dance,
Lost in the magic of sweet romance.

Through time we sail on tranquil seas,
With every wave, a sighing breeze.
Memories linger like autumn's gold,
In every touch, a tale retold.

Love Letters to the Infinite

In every star, a letter lies,
Written in whispers, across the skies.
With ink of passion, eternal and bold,
Our love inscribed in silver and gold.

Through timeless realms where dreams take flight,
We pen our hearts in endless night.
Each word a beacon, bright and clear,
A testament to all we hold dear.

The Diary of Every Embrace

In whispers soft beneath the stars,
We find a warmth that time forgets.
Each moment pressed, a fleeting pulse,
A tapestry of whispered debts.

With every hug, a story spun,
Of laughter shared and tears unseen.
A book of love, where pages turn,
In every clasp, you reign supreme.

The ink may fade, but hearts remain,
Your scent, a ghost entwined with mine.
In shadows where our secrets lay,
Each hug a verse, each sigh a line.

So let us write through years uncharted,
In every embrace, a chance to feel.
The diary filled with heartbeats treasured,
In arms that dance, our fate is sealed.

The Lexicon of Longing Dreams

In moonlit nights where wishes dwell,
I sketch your name in silver beams.
A language born of heartbeats fast,
Composed in whispers of our dreams.

Through silent paths of blurred desires,
I wander deep, yet stay awake.
Each heartbeat speaks a million words,
A lexicon, which we must make.

In colors bright that paint the sky,
Your smile ignites a world anew.
In longing dreams, our souls align,
With every breath, I'm drawn to you.

Let every wish be inked in stars,
From distant realms, our voices stream.
In the twilight's hold, I'll find you here,
The lexicon of longing dreams.

Insignia of a Timeless Bond

In woven threads of fate we meet,
An insignia, bold and bright.
In every glance, a promise passed,
A bond that glows, a guiding light.

Through years that whisper soft and low,
I wear your laughter like a crown.
Each moment shared, a jewel found,
In echoes where love won't back down.

The compass points to gentle shores,
Where hands unite, where hearts are free.
In every fold of shared silence,
The insignia crafted in you and me.

For time may stretch and life may change,
Yet through the storms, we keep our song.
In timeless grace, our spirits dance,
An insignia of love's lifelong throng.

Resonance in Unspoken Words

In glances wrapped in tender space,
A language found without a sound.
The heartbeat echoes, pulses race,
In silence, deeper truths abound.

With every sigh, a story brews,
In quiet moments, dreams entwine.
Resonance lingers in our core,
In unspoken realms, your heart is mine.

Through years of silence, fortunes found,
A depth to love, profound and wide.
In body language, we are lost,
In gestures small, our hearts collide.

Let not the words betray the bond,
For in the hush, our spirits play.
In resonance of love's sweet song,
Unspoken words weave night and day.

The Language of Unseen Bonds

In whispers soft, we find our way,
Through silent glances, hearts do sway.
Each note we share, a gentle thread,
In shadows deep, our secrets spread.

The hands that reach, though miles apart,
Compose a song, a work of art.
With every sigh, a tale unfolds,
A tapestry of love retold.

Within the Crypt of Affection

Amidst the stones, where memories lie,
We carve our names, as time drifts by.
In quiet corners, shadows blend,
An echo of the love we send.

The warmth of touch, a fleeting breath,
Transcends the bounds of whispered death.
In every heart, a lantern glows,
Illuminating paths we chose.

Unraveled Threads of Emotion

A tangled web of dreams and fears,
Each thread reveals what time endears.
In moments shared, we come alive,
Through laughter's glow, our spirits strive.

With every tear, a story weeps,
In silence bold, our heartache keeps.
The fabric worn, our souls entwined,
In every loss, a love defined.

The Silent Alphabet of Yearning

In muted vows, our wishes bloom,
A language carved in twilight's gloom.
Each pause we take, a thought conveyed,
A heartfelt sigh, when words have strayed.

The yearning gaze, a secret told,
In fleeting glances, warmth unfolds.
We spell our hopes in silent ink,
In dreams we weave, we dare to think.

Writings of the Unseen

In shadows where whispers dwell,
Silent tales start to swell.
Ink flows like a gentle stream,
Capturing a distant dream.

Words dance on the edge of sight,
Carving paths in the night.
Secrets cloaked, yet they sing,
Of the truth that silence brings.

Traces of Enigmatic Longing

Footprints lost in shifting sand,
Echoes of a gentle hand.
Heartbeats blend in every sigh,
Where yearning shadows lie.

In a realm that feels divine,
Whispers mingle, intertwine.
Longing holds a fragile thread,
Binding all that's left unsaid.

Silhouettes of Unvoiced Feelings

In twilight's soft embrace,
Shadows take a hidden place.
Emotions whisper, unexpressed,
Carved in silence, ever pressed.

Eyes reflect what lips can't share,
A language woven in the air.
In every glance, a story flows,
Where unvoiced love softly glows.

Layers of the Soul's Codex

Beneath the surface, mysteries lie,
Veils of longing, floating high.
Each layer holds a gentle truth,
Guarding echoes of lost youth.

Through time's gentle bending arc,
Wisdom glimmers in the dark.
Each story, etched in silent flight,
Guides us through the depths of night.

Heartbeats in Hieratic Forms

In shadows deep where whispers dwell,
Ancient signs that hearts can tell.
Each pulse a mark, a silent song,
In the night where dreams belong.

With every beat, the ink flows bright,
Eternal dance in silver light.
Hieratic forms in tender glow,
Speaking truths we yearn to know.

In every stroke, a love displayed,
Hidden hopes and fears arrayed.
With every heartbeat, stories cling,
In these forms, our souls take wing.

Inward Languages of Love

Listen close to the silent sound,
Where hearts connect without a bound.
A glance, a touch, all else fades,
In inward languages, love cascades.

Each unspoken word, a soft embrace,
In secret rooms, our sacred space.
With gentle sighs, we weave and bind,
A tapestry of souls entwined.

In every pause, a world revealed,
Through whispered dreams, our fate is sealed.
In quiet moments, love takes flight,
A language formed in pure delight.

The Cipher of Connection

In every glance, a code untold,
A cipher crafted in the bold.
Unraveling layers, we dare explore,
The depths of souls we both adore.

With every heartbeat, signals trace,
Mapping networks in boundless space.
A dance of minds, a spark ignites,
As hidden paths align in lights.

Through words unspoken, we convey,
The mysteries of love's array.
In shared silence, we find release,
A cipher's strength, a bond of peace.

Sorrow Scrawled in Soft Light

In twilight shades, the sorrow clings,
Scrawled in whispers, the heartstrings.
Each tear a tale, a lingering ache,
In soft light's glow, we bend, we break.

With every sigh, a spirit's weight,
Framed in shadows, we contemplate.
Through fragile moments, pain takes flight,
In the crevices of fading light.

But through the sorrow, we find the way,
To dance in dusk, embrace the gray.
For even in loss, a lesson stays,
Scrawled in soft light, life's gentle maze.

Declarations in the Quiet Hours

In the hushed whispers of night,
Promises form in the still air.
Hearts beating softly in time,
Hope dances like shadows, bare.

Moonlight spills secrets of love,
Every sigh a gentle plea.
Time slows in the quiet pines,
Under stars, just you and me.

Echoes of dreams drift like smoke,
Carried on winds of the calm.
In the dark, our souls align,
Wrapped in night's tender balm.

Such moments, pure and profound,
Live in the silence we share.
Declarations of a deep bond,
In the quiet, our hearts laid bare.

Secrets Embedded in the Pulse

Beneath the skin, rhythms flow,
Each heartbeat a tale to tell.
Whispers linger, truths unfold,
In the pulse, our secrets dwell.

Fingers brush, electric touch,
Time freezes in this embrace.
Unspoken words, tangled thoughts,
In the silence, we find grace.

Moments fade, yet linger on,
Echoes of laughter and sighs.
Memories weave like soft threads,
In our hearts, love never dies.

Hidden depths, we navigate,
With every stroke and glance,
The secrets we hold together,
Are the rhythm of our dance.

Sorrows Etched in Ekphrasis

Colors bleed on the canvas,
Each brushstroke a tear in time.
Silence speaks in muted hues,
Sorrow pours in every rhyme.

Figures trapped in frames of pain,
Stories captured in cold light.
Echoes of lost dreams linger,
In the dark, we find the fight.

Fragmented thoughts whisper low,
Artistry holds hearts in thrall.
In the gallery of our loss,
Every heartbeat stands so tall.

Yet within the aching lines,
Resilience paints shades of hope.
Sorrows etched in ekphrasis,
Through the art, we learn to cope.

Timelines Intertwined with Affection

In the dance of fleeting moments,
Paths converge and then collide.
Time's tapestry, richly woven,
In your gaze, I find my guide.

Every hour, every season,
Threads of fate, we gently trace.
With each smile, a new beginning,
In this love, we find our place.

Past and present merge as one,
Softly stitched with tender care.
Timelines lead us to forever,
In the stories that we share.

Through the years, through the laughter,
Memories become our song.
Timelines intertwined with affection,
In this journey, we belong.

The Language of Beating Hues

In twilight's brush, the colors blend,
A canvas wakes, where shadows bend.
Whispers dance on every hue,
Each stroke a voice, both bright and blue.

From crimson hearts to emerald sighs,
The paintings speak, where silence lies.
A symphony of shades in play,
The art of love in bright array.

Impression of Uncharted Affection

In secret glances, hearts collide,
A map unfolds, paths yet untried.
Each fleeting moment paints the sky,
With shades of dreams where spirits fly.

Soft echoes linger in the air,
The brush of fate, a whispered dare.
Each unturned leaf holds stories dear,
Of tender fears and fleeting cheer.

Secrets Scrawled in Forgotten Corners

In dusty nooks where past resides,
Are tales of love the heart confides.
With every mark, a story lives,
Of whispered truths the silence gives.

A hidden world 'neath layers deep,
Where quiet secrets dare to weep.
Through cobwebs spun and shadows cast,
The echoes of a love that lasts.

The Palette of Inner Sentiments

With strokes of joy and shades of pain,
Life's canvas shifts in sun and rain.
Each color born from joy or strife,
A brilliant mix that paints our life.

The hues of pride, of hope, and fear,
Crafting stories that each soul can hear.
In every blend, a truth revealed,
The palette's heart, forever sealed.

Dialogues Found in Breaths

In whispered winds we find our tone,
Echoes caress the hearts we own.
Each breath a promise softly made,
Words unspoken, yet never swayed.

A dance of sighs beneath the stars,
Conversations held from afar.
Silent laughter in the night,
As shadows weave our shared delight.

Invisible Patterns of Embrace

In twilight's hue, our souls align,
Creating patterns, yours and mine.
The gentle pull of unseen ties,
A tapestry of soft goodbyes.

Within the void, we find our space,
Wrapped in warmth, a sweet embrace.
Fingers trace the air, so light,
Mapping dreams in the still of night.

The Cartouches of Desire

Inscribed in time, our wishes glow,
Cartouches made of joy and woe.
Desire dances on the page,
In ancient scripts, we find our stage.

Whispers linger like fragrant blooms,
Filling air with sweet perfumes.
Ink flows boldly, secrets shared,
In every curve, a heart laid bare.

The Harmonics of Unsung Dreams

In shadows cast by silver beams,
Lie the harmonics of dreams unseen.
A symphony of whispered hopes,
Resonating where silence copes.

Soft echoes play upon the strings,
Awakening the joy life brings.
In every chord, the heart will soar,
With unsung melodies we explore.

Whispers of Inward Secrets

In shadows deep, the whispers dwell,
Veiled in silence, they softly tell.
The heart keeps secrets, safe and sound,
In gentle echoes, the truths are found.

Beneath the surface, layers lie,
A world unseen beneath the sky.
Tender murmurs in the night,
Guide us home, through dark to light.

Each breath a tale, each sigh a clue,
A dance of thoughts, just me and you.
With every heartbeat, we unfold,
In whispers soft, our souls are told.

So let the silence speak its grace,
In hidden realms, we find our place.
With whispered dreams and tender care,
In inward secrets, we lay bare.

Veils of Emotion Unraveled

In layers thin, emotions hide,
Behind the veil, our hopes reside.
Each thread a story, delicate spun,
In tangled hearts, the battles won.

Bright colors flare, then fade away,
What once was bold, turns shades of gray.
Yet deep beneath, the passion flows,
In every heartbeat, it fiercely grows.

Truths bound tightly, fears set free,
Unraveled paths, a mystery.
We strip the layers, one by one,
To find the warmth of the setting sun.

In twilight's glow, our spirits soar,
As veils fall back, we crave for more.
With every pulse, a tale unveiled,
In emotions' depths, our lives are scaled.

The Code Beneath Our Feelings

In silent codes, our hearts engage,
Deciphering love from every page.
A language soft, with tender grace,
In every look, a warm embrace.

Beneath the words, the truth resides,
In hidden glances, love confides.
A script that flows like rivers bend,
In every sigh, our hearts commend.

With every heartbeat, we compile,
The secrets shared, a knowing smile.
A puzzle crafted in the dark,
With every piece, we leave our mark.

So let us write in ink of gold,
The stories of us, forever told.
In lines entwined, the code reveals,
The deeper pulse of what love feels.

Silent Scripts of Passion

In quiet rooms, desire dwells,
A language spoken without spells.
Each glance a word, each breath a line,
In silent scripts, our souls entwine.

The night unfolds, a canvas bare,
Where shadows paint the secrets we share.
With every touch, a story born,
In whispered dreams, our hearts adorn.

The silence sings, a sweet refrain,
In passion's grip, we feel the gain.
Our bodies dance, in quiet flight,
Across the canvas of the night.

So hush your thoughts and let them flow,
In silent scripts, our love will grow.
With every pause, a moment stays,
In passion's ink, we write our ways.

Code of Celestial Encounters

Stars whisper secrets at night,
Constellations weave timeless tales.
Galaxies dance in a silent flight,
Fading light, where wonder prevails.

Planets align in cosmic grace,
Waves of stardust gently flow.
Each heartbeat charts a tender space,
As above, so below, we grow.

Nebulas cradle ancient dreams,
In the dark, a spark ignites.
Through the vastness, hope redeems,
Guiding souls through endless nights.

In the silence, love's echo sings,
Like meteors tracing skies undone.
In every glance, a universe clings,
Two spirits merge; they are as one.

The Script of Shared Solitude

In corners of hearts, shadows blend,
Words linger softly in the air.
Solitude calls, a quiet friend,
A space where thoughts are laid bare.

Pages turn, the ink unfolds,
Stories written in silence profound.
Through whispered dreams, a truth behold,
In solitude's grace, we are found.

Moments echo, time stands still,
Between breaths, a glimmering pause.
In shared silence, we feel the thrill,
Binding hearts without a cause.

A tapestry woven, tender threads,
In each heartbeat, a promise is made.
Together alone, where comfort spreads,
In shared solitude, we are laid.

Portraits of Unarticulated Desires

In the silence, longing stirs,
Fleeting glances, unspoken dreams.
Canvas of hope, where truth occurs,
Brushstrokes of passion's gentle beams.

Eyes meet shyly, worlds collide,
Echoes of fire in hollowed hearts.
In the shadows, love can't hide,
Each glance a masterpiece that starts.

Whispers of wishes paint the night,
Every breath, a canvas anew.
Emotion lingers, soft and light,
In the heart, where art breaks through.

The gallery of what could be,
Each frame a story wrapped in sighs.
In unarticulated symphony,
Desires dance beneath the skies.

The Luminous Palimpsest of Feelings

Layers of love etched in time,
History's hands hold us close.
Whispers of joy, a rhythmic rhyme,
In every heartbeat, a silent prose.

Memories shine, like stars at dusk,
Infinite tales on parchment fade.
In the warmth, we find our musk,
The essence of feelings displayed.

In shadows cast by fleeting light,
Emotions swirl, a vivid dance.
Through the night, we take our flight,
In the palimpsest, we find our chance.

Luminous threads weave through the dark,
Binding moments, fragile and bright.
In every heartbeat, a love's spark,
In the layers, we find our light.

Glyphs of Longing and Yearning

In shadows deep, the whispers grow,
Carved in dreams, the secrets flow.
A heart that aches, a soul that roams,
Where echoes call, we seek our homes.

Fingers trace the lines of fate,
In twilight hours, we hesitate.
With every breath, the longing swells,
In silent nights, the yearning dwells.

Stars align in patterns clear,
Through twilight haze, we draw them near.
Each fleeting gaze, a promise made,
In every thought, the past is laid.

Yet still we chase the fading light,
In solemn dreams, we reunite.
For glyphs of hope forever weave,
A tapestry of love believe.

Mysteries Etched in Silence

In the hush of night, secrets bloom,
Whispers linger, a veiled gloom.
Shadows dance, a silent song,
Where hidden truths will soon belong.

Time holds its breath, still as stone,
Each moment hangs, a muted tone.
We search for answers in the dark,
Lost in dreams, we leave a mark.

Every glance, a story told,
In silence wrapped, treasures unfold.
Mysteries etched in quiet grace,
Reveal reflections we embrace.

Yet when dawn breaks, light reveals,
The beating heart that slowly heals.
In whispers soft, our souls atone,
In silence shared, we're never alone.

Scribes of Desire

With ink of dreams, we write our fate,
Scribes of desire, hearts palpitate.
Words unspoken linger like dusk,
In tender tones, a whispered husk.

Each line is drawn with fervent hope,
In every pause, the spirits cope.
A parchment worn, the tales unfold,
Of passions fierce and hearts of gold.

With every stroke, our yearnings blend,
In twilight hues, beginnings end.
The quill caresses, a gentle touch,
We seek companionship, we crave so much.

In the silence, promises reside,
With open hearts, we turn the tide.
For scribes of desire forever write,
In love's embrace, we find our light.

Patterns of the Unspoken

Beneath the stars, a dance divine,
Patterns speak, though words entwine.
In glances shared, the silence sings,
While hearts align, as fate's bell rings.

With every step, we weave the thread,
In cosmic patterns, our souls are led.
The unspoken bonds, so deeply sewn,
In every breath, the truth is known.

Nature's rhythm, a sacred beat,
In quiet spaces, our worlds meet.
Each heartbeat echoes, whispers flow,
In midnight tales, the spirits know.

For in the silence, stories bloom,
Creating light amidst the gloom.
Patterns etched in every trace,
In unbroken trust, we find our place.

Echoes of Love's Ancient Script

In whispered tones beneath the stars,
We trace the lines of fate and scars.
Each note a promise, soft and sweet,
In the dance of hearts, our souls retreat.

The parchment holds our secrets dear,
In shadows cast, we shed our fear.
With every heartbeat, time stands still,
For love, my dear, is purest will.

Through storms and calm, we carve our path,
In laughter's glow, we find the math.
Two bodies merge, as one they sing,
A symphony of joy we bring.

So here's our tale, in ink and light,
An echo through the endless night.
With every breath, we write our verse,
In love, each moment we immerse.

Veils of Unspoken Desires

Behind a smile, what words remain?
In silence deep, we feel the pain.
A glance exchanged, ignites the flame,
Yet still we play the waiting game.

The air is thick with unshared thoughts,
In every heart, a battle fought.
A brush of hands, a fleeting glance,
In shadows deep, we find our dance.

These veils we wear, our secret shield,
In quiet moments, truth revealed.
To tread the line, between the light,
A longing felt, yet out of sight.

With every breath, the tension grows,
Awakening, what no one knows.
The beauty lies in what we lack,
In unspoken words, we find our track.

Inked in the Language of Longing

With ink of dreams, we script our fate,
Each stroke a hope, each pause a wait.
In letters penned by candle's glow,
Our desires dance, our feelings flow.

From distant shores, our voices call,
In every letter, we risk it all.
The language speaks of hearts entwined,
A written truth, our souls aligned.

Though distance claims its heavy price,
With every word, we roll the dice.
For in these pages, life is drawn,
Inked in the love that lingers on.

So let us write till ink runs dry,
With every tear, with every sigh.
In the language of longing, love's refrain,
We find our peace, we know no pain.

Shadows of the Soul's Codex

In silence wrapped, the shadows play,
Unlocking doors to yesterday.
A hidden tale in every sigh,
Where whispers breathe, and spirits fly.

The codex waits for hearts to seek,
In every line, the truth we speak.
With gentle ink, the past unfolds,
A tapestry of dreams retold.

As twilight fades, our secrets bloom,
In twilight's hush, dispelling gloom.
These shadows guide, where light can't tread,
To realms of love, where angels tread.

So here we stand, in twilight's glow,
In shadows deep, our souls will flow.
With every heartbeat, trust is found,
In soul's codex, we're forever bound.

Inscriptions of Forgotten Emotions

Whispers cling to shadows wide,
Fleeting dreams where secrets hide.
Faded ink on yellowed page,
Unveiling hearts in sorrow's cage.

Tears that linger in the night,
Promises lost, out of sight.
Echoes of a lover's sigh,
Inscriptions that will never die.

Silent hopes in twilight's glow,
Memories that ebb and flow.
Familiar touch that slipped away,
Yet still they haunt, refuse to sway.

Each emotion, a story told,
In the quiet, brave and bold.
Forgotten ink upon the skin,
Tales of love where pain begins.

Cartographer of the Soul's Echo

Lines mapped out through every tear,
Marking paths that led us here.
With each heartbeat, a new trail,
In the silence, soft winds wail.

Stars above, they guide the way,
In the darkness, night meets day.
Charting dreams that drift afar,
With every heartbeat, every scar.

Whispers chart the winding road,
In the depths, the light bestowed.
Guiding souls through thick and thin,
Maps we craft to find within.

Every echo, a voice in time,
Drawing lines in rhythm and rhyme.
Cartographer of what is felt,
In the heart, the compass dwelt.

Glyphs that Speak in Silence

Symbols etched upon the mind,
Secrets hidden, hard to find.
Every gaze, a story spun,
Words unspoken, yet they run.

Silent whispers fill the air,
Glyphs emerge from deep despair.
In the shadows, truths collide,
In their presence, hearts abide.

Tales of love, of loss entwined,
Echoes of what once was kind.
In the stillness, voices breathe,
Glyphs that speak, refusing leave.

Let the ink flow, soft and pure,
In silence, find the only cure.
Each glyph a tale, a quiet plea,
In the void, we seek to be.

Patterns Carved by Time's Hand

Waves of fate, they rise and fall,
Time etches marks upon us all.
Lines of joy, of pain entwined,
In the fabric, truths defined.

Moments passed, like grains of sand,
Patterns formed by fate's own hand.
Each heartbeat leaves a trace,
In the quiet, we find grace.

Stories woven, threads of gold,
In these patterns, life unfolds.
Chasing shadows, grasping light,
Carved by time in day and night.

Nature sings a lullaby,
With each moment, we comply.
Patterns shift but never cease,
In time's embrace, we find peace.

Markings of a Celestial Connection

In whispers of the night sky,
Stars weave tales of our fate,
Faint lights dance and collide,
A map written in cosmic weight.

Beneath the moon's soft embrace,
Our shadows merge and align,
Each heartbeat a distant trace,
Time blurs, love's endless sign.

Galaxies drift in our gaze,
Gravity pulls at our souls,
Celestial bodies ablaze,
Together, we fill the holes.

A comet's tail paints the air,
With each flicker, feelings rise,
In the vastness, we both dare,
To chase the light in our eyes.

The Undeciphered Map of Touch

Fingers trace the lines of fate,
Skin maps scenes of unspoken dreams,
Each brush a new, open gate,
In silence, love's spirit beams.

Guided by the warmth we share,
Paths entwined, we journey deep,
Lost in moments, nothing's rare,
The secrets our bodies keep.

Hints of longing linger near,
Every touch a silent scream,
In the tension, love cohere,
As reality meets the dream.

Through the darkness, hands will find,
In the chaos, we create,
A language only we defined,
Innocent yet so innate.

Crumbs of Sentiment in the Dark

In the shadow, whispers blend,
Fleeting glances spark the night,
Scattered echoes softly mend,
Hearts search for a guiding light.

Every sigh, a breadcrumb trail,
Leading back to where you are,
Trusting in the love we hail,
Navigating by the stars.

Silhouettes in muted tones,
Crafting warmth from cool despair,
Life's rich tapestry intones,
Each fragment shows how we care.

In this twilight, we confide,
Painting dreams in midnight hues,
Through the dark, we will abide,
Finding joy in all we lose.

Hidden Emblems of Tenderness

In moments soft as morning dew,
Gentle gestures speak of grace,
Each glance a promise, pure and true,
Holding treasures time won't erase.

In laughter shared, we intertwine,
Zippers of souls gently exposed,
Every heartbeat feels divine,
As the light of love transposed.

Silent symbols etched in time,
Guardians of our sweet embrace,
Words unspoken, yet they chime,
Echoes of our sacred space.

In every secret glance we share,
Tenderness remains our art,
Hidden emblems laid with care,
Crafted deep within the heart.

The Manuscript of Sighs

In shadows where whispers dwell,
Page by page, our secrets swell.
Ink of dreams, both faint and clear,
Each sigh a story, drawn near.

Lost in the echoes of the heart,
Words unspoken, yet they part.
Bated breaths on parchment lie,
An endless manuscript of sighs.

Every flutter, a gentle breeze,
Binding memories with such ease.
In twilight hours, thoughts cascade,
A written world that won't soon fade.

As we pen, the night ignites,
With silent songs, our hearts take flight.
Through ink and dreams, we travel far,
Carving our fate beneath each star.

Heartstrings and Hieroglyphics

In the tapestry of time we weave,
Heartstrings sing, but few believe.
Hieroglyphics etched in skin,
Stories of love where we begin.

Each note a whisper, soft and low,
Melodies of where we go.
Symbols dancing in the air,
Mapping out the love we share.

Through ancient echoes, truth unfolds,
Tales of warmth against the cold.
Every glance a coded line,
In this language, hearts entwine.

Together we paint the unseen,
In colors bright where dreams convene.
With every beat, life rolls and bends,
A symphony that never ends.

Secrets Scripted in Stardust

In the quiet of the night sky,
Whispers linger, soft as sighs.
Stardust glimmers, tales untold,
Secrets waiting to unfold.

Galaxies twirl, a dance divine,
Each grain a shimmer, a hidden line.
Within the cosmos, wishes blend,
Heartfelt echoes that never end.

Dreams interwoven with twinkling light,
Navigating through the endless night.
Each secret penned in silver glow,
A transient truth, a cosmic flow.

As we wish upon this dream,
Silent stardust starts to gleam.
An infinite message in every star,
Binding our spirits, no matter how far.

The Ephemeral Art of Connection

In fleeting moments, we collide,
Hearts unveiled, with nothing to hide.
Connections made in whispers soft,
Building bridges that lift us aloft.

Each glance exchanged, a silent spark,
Illuminating shadows in the dark.
Ephemeral threads that bind and weave,
In the tapestry of love, we believe.

With every heartbeat, stories flow,
A dance of souls that gently glow.
In laughter's echo or a shared sigh,
We find the reasons, learn to fly.

Though moments fade like morning mist,
The art of connection will persist.
In the gallery of time, we'll see,
The beauty of what it means to be.

Sculpted Silences of the Affectionate

In quiet rooms where whispers dwell,
Hearts converse without a sound,
Hands entwined, a sacred spell,
In sculpted silences, love's profound.

Eyes that speak, a tender gaze,
Each moment hangs, a breath of peace,
In this embrace, the world does fade,
For in our stillness, joy's release.

The softest touch, a gentle brush,
Time pauses here, just you and me,
In silent vows, we know the rush,
Of love adorned in mystery.

Together in this cherished space,
The quiet hum of hearts aligned,
In sculpted silences, we trace,
A love that's timeless and enshrined.

The Codex of Heartfelt Echoes

In pages worn by tender grips,
Our laughter written, joy unfurled,
Through every line, love's sweet eclipse,
The codex of our secret world.

Memories inked in shades of gold,
Whispers caught in endless loops,
Each heartbeat tells a story bold,
In echoes where our passion scoops.

With every chapter, dreams take flight,
The bridge of trust, a steadfast bind,
In the margins, hope ignites,
The codex of two hearts combined.

In twilight hues, we turn the page,
A journey held in timeless grace,
In every word, love's quiet stage,
The echoes of our warm embrace.

Love's Uncharted Cartography

Across the seas of unclaimed hearts,
We map the stars, our guiding light,
Through every glance, a world imparts,
Love's uncharted cartography, our flight.

In valleys deep, where shadows play,
We sketch our dreams on endless skies,
With compass hearts, we find a way,
To navigate through soft goodbyes.

Each moment shared, a dot we draw,
A treasure found, a path defined,
With every sigh, we break the law,
Of distance held by love enshrined.

With endless maps of places new,
We chart our course through every storm,
In love's embrace, we always knew,
Adventure waits, our hearts keep warm.

Symbols in the Silence of Night

Under the stars, where shadows sigh,
We find the symbols of our dreams,
In quiet spaces, hearts comply,
With whispered truths that softly beam.

The moonlight paints our secrets bright,
A canvas stretched with silver threads,
In the stillness of the night,
Our souls unravel, love is spread.

Hand in hand, we cast our wishes,
In silent prayers, we seek the sky,
Each twinkling star, a heart that swishes,
In the silence, love can fly.

With every breath, a story told,
In symbols of the night, we find,
The whispers of our hearts, so bold,
In silence, love is intertwined.

Signposts of Inner Landscapes

In quiet glades where shadows play,
Leaves whisper truths, old and gray.
A path unfolds in gentle light,
Marking journeys beyond our sight.

Rivers flow with tales untold,
In their depths, the heart is bold.
Mountains rise to touch the sky,
Carrying dreams that never die.

Each step leads to unseen shores,
Where reflections breathe, and spirit soars.
Past the veils of fear and doubt,
Hope emerges, one heart, one shout.

In the silence, listen near,
The signposts guide, the way is clear.
With every turn, a story blooms,
Unfolding life in vibrant rooms.

Reflections in the Heart's Mirror

Glistening waters hold the truth,
Fragments of love, echoes of youth.
In stillness, faces dance and weave,
Softly whispering what we believe.

Mirrors crack yet hold the light,
Shattered pieces, a fragile sight.
Within each shard, a voice will sing,
The timeless joy that memories bring.

Hidden beneath, the stories lie,
Silent dreams that yearn to fly.
Glimmers of hope in every gaze,
Reflecting life in myriad ways.

Through the glass, we seek and find,
Connections forged, heart aligned.
In every ripple, a lesson clear,
Reflections echo, drawing near.

Whispers of Unsung Symbols

In shadows cast by ancient trees,
Whispers linger on the breeze.
Symbols carved in bark and stone,
Tell of journeys not yet known.

The moonlight weaves through tangled leaves,
A tapestry of what deceives.
Hidden signs in the twilight hum,
Calling forth what's yet to come.

In silence speaks a distant hymn,
Unseen worlds on horizons brim.
The heartbeats thrum like sacred drums,
Echoing tales of those who comes.

Under stars, the secrets glow,
Guiding souls in ebb and flow.
Through whispered truths, we find our way,
In the depth of night, where shadows play.

Secrets Beneath the Flesh

In tender skin, the stories hide,
Layers deep where dreams abide.
Every scar, a tale profound,
Beneath the flesh, life spins around.

Veins pulse with memories past,
Echoes of a vibrant cast.
Every heartbeat, a silent plea,
For understanding, to be free.

Softly spoken, the body knows,
Secrets mingling in highs and lows.
A dance of pain, a waltz of grace,
In every line, we find our place.

Beneath the surface, truth ignites,
In shadows lost, the soul alights.
Through the flesh, we seek and learn,
Discovering what we crave in turn.

The Annotation of Shared Glances

In the crowd, our eyes meet,
A fleeting whisper, so discreet.
Words unspoken, yet so clear,
In that moment, you are near.

Memories etched in silence,
Suspended time, a dance of chance.
With every glance, a story spun,
Underneath the fading sun.

Emotions flicker, soft and bright,
Painting shadows in the night.
Tales of laughter, hints of tears,
A tapestry woven through the years.

Each gaze a note, a silent tune,
Echoing softly, like the moon.
In the stillness, we both know,
The language of love, gentle glow.

Syllables of Silence in the Past

Whispers linger, hushed and low,
In the corners where memories grow.
Syllables echo, soft and meek,
The stories shared, the words we seek.

Time stands still, a sacred pause,
In every silence, a hidden cause.
Fragments of laughter, tears once shed,
In the silence, the words unsaid.

Layers of moments, bittersweet,
In the quiet, our hearts repeat.
Years may fade, but truths remain,
In syllables lost, love's refrain.

A canvas painted in soft gray,
Unwritten verses, night and day.
In the silence, our souls align,
With every heartbeat, your heart is mine.

Inkwells of Affection's Age

Inkwells deep, the stories flow,
Love inscribes what hearts both know.
Each letter penned with tender grace,
In the margins, our hearts embrace.

Time wears on, but ink remains,
Capturing joy, the sweetest pains.
Every stroke, a fleeting glance,
Written whispers of our romance.

Pages turn, the seasons change,
Yet our love, it will not age.
Through ink and paper, we ignite,
A world alive in black and white.

In every word, a promise stays,
In the inkwell, love's gentle rays.
Etched in time, we'll always be,
Together, writing our history.

Dialogues Beyond the Surface

Beneath the words, a current flows,
In the space where silence grows.
We speak in glances, soft and wise,
In this language, truth never lies.

Dialogues drift on the breeze,
Rustling leaves, the sound of ease.
With every heartbeat, whispers start,
Conversations penned within the heart.

Layers peel back, revealing light,
In the depths, we soar, take flight.
Beyond the surface, the depths invite,
Each phrase a dance, a pure delight.

Connection forged in quiet spheres,
A bond that resonates through years.
In dialogues, our souls conspire,
Together igniting love's true fire.

Ancestral Chords of Emotion

In the silent woods, echoes reside,
Threads of the past, woven with pride.
Ancestors call through whispers of time,
Their stories alive in rhythm and rhyme.

Hearts beat in tune with the earth's gentle sigh,
Roots interlace, reaching for the sky.
Memories linger like shadows at dusk,
Binding our fates in a mystical husk.

Tales of old sung through the breeze,
Carried afar by rustling leaves.
Each tear, each laugh, a note played in space,
An ode to the past in this sacred place.

Sewn in our spirits, these chords intertwine,
Strumming the fabric where souls align.
With every heartbeat, in unity's grace,
A symphony blooms in this timeless embrace.

The Sign Language of Souls

In the hush of the night, fingers dance free,
Painting the air, a silent decree.
Emotions unbound, beyond words they flow,
In gestures so soft, hearts come to know.

Eyes speak a language, deep and profound,
Connecting the souls without making a sound.
A glance, a flick, a touch of the hand,
Ties we have woven, perfectly planned.

Unraveled secrets in every embrace,
Life pulses through touch, a warm, sacred space.
In the silence shared, worlds collide,
The sign language whispers where truths cannot hide.

Each moment alive with expressive grace,
Love's quiet notes in this intimate place.
Hands sketch the stories our hearts long to tell,
In the sign language of souls, everything dwells.

Portraits in the Language of Touch

Fingers trace contours, a story is drawn,
In the soft light of dusk, where strangers can yawn.
A brush of the skin speaks volumes unheard,
Painting emotions with each tender word.

The warmth of a hand, the strength of a grasp,
Silent expressions in a fleeting clasp.
A caress that lingers, like time standing still,
Embracing the pulse of a shared, gentle thrill.

Textures of longing, woven in lace,
Crafting a gallery in the quiet space.
Each meeting of hands, a vibrant brush stroke,
Creating a portrait where silence awoke.

Capturing hearts in a canvas so wide,
A gallery formed by what's deep inside.
In the language of touch, we find our release,
Crafting portraits of love, infused with peace.

Whispers Woven into Emotions

In a garden of thoughts, softly they bloom,
Whispers like petals dispel the gloom.
Fragrant with secrets, sweet and profound,
Carried on winds, in soft sighs they're found.

Voices of echoes, like ripples on lakes,
Awakening feelings that softly awakes.
Each murmur a thread, weaving through dreams,
Stitching our hearts with delicate seams.

A whisper of hope, a song of despair,
Tales of connection that float in the air.
In the quiet of moments, emotions unfold,
Woven together, a tapestry bold.

As stars whisper secrets from high above,
We listen in stillness, wrapped in pure love.
In the tapestry of life, rich and complete,
Whispers of emotions make us whole, make us sweet.

The Cartographer's Heart

Through valleys deep and mountains high,
The lines of love reach towards the sky.
With ink of dreams, my map is drawn,
A journey starts with every dawn.

In every curve, in every twist,
My heart beats strong, it can't resist.
The compass guides where feelings flow,
In every step, I learn to grow.

Each landmark holds a whispered tale,
Of hopes and fears that softly sail.
The cartographer within me sighs,
As I trace paths beneath the skies.

So take my hand, let's chart the stars,
Mapping love, despite the scars.
With every stroke, the world expands,
The cartographer dreams, our hearts in hands.

Expressions Stitched in Shadows

In twilight's loom, where whispers weave,
In shadows dark, we choose to believe.
With threads of hope, they intertwine,
Creating art that feels divine.

Each secret stitch, a story told,
Of warmth and courage, brave and bold.
Expressions dance in softest night,
We find our strength, we claim our light.

They wrap around the fragile heart,
Binding the pieces, each a part.
In shadowed corners, dreams ignite,
As we embrace the quiet fight.

So let us craft with gentle hands,
In every fold, a love that stands.
Stitched together, we will shine,
In shadows deep, our souls align.

Memories Inscribed in Stone

Ancient echoes carved so deep,
In stone we find the past we keep.
Each chisel's mark a tale of old,
Of love, of loss, and dreams retold.

These faded words, they speak to me,
In silence, they set memories free.
Through time they stand, steadfast and true,
In every grain, a glimpse of you.

A monument to fleeting days,
As shadows dance in soft sun rays.
With every touch, a world awakes,
In stone we find what time remakes.

So let us honor those who came,
Their stories carved, their hearts aflame.
In memories etched, we find our place,
A legacy in Earth's embrace.

Preliminary Scribes of Connection

With ink and paper, hearts align,
In scribbled words, our thoughts entwine.
A glance, a smile, a silent nod,
In every moment, we find the God.

Preliminary notes of tender grace,
In letters shared, we find our space.
With every line, a bond begins,
In quiet whispers, the warmth of kin.

Together drafting paths to find,
The echoes of our hearts combined.
In every stroke, connection grows,
Through written lines, affection flows.

So let our words be bridges strong,
Uniting souls where they belong.
In pens we find the sparks ignite,
Preliminary scribes of pure delight.

Enigmas Written in Blood

Ink stains on parchment, secrets bleed,
Whispers of shadows, a treacherous creed.
Beneath the surface, riddles entwine,
Lurking in darkness, the truth's hard to find.

Strokes of the pen, tracing the fate,
A thrum of the heart, a life in debate.
Veins carry stories, tales left untold,
The weight of the ink, the fire of bold.

Silent confessions in the night air,
A canvas of crimson, secrets laid bare.
In every letter, a passion ignites,
Each word a dagger, love's haunting bites.

Enigmas arise, like smoke from the flame,
Etched in the silence, they'll never be tamed.
Blood spills the secrets, a fate intertwined,
Echoes of heartbeats, forever combined.

Heartstrings and Ancient Symbols

Woven like threads, our heartstrings align,
Each pulse in rhythm, a sacred design.
Ancient symbols whisper, binding us tight,
In the tapestry woven, love's gentle light.

With hands in the soil, roots intertwine,
Cultivating dreams on this sacred line.
Letters and glyphs, a language divine,
Eons of love, in starlight we shine.

The heart knows the dance, a celestial waltz,
In twilight's embrace, no fear, nor faults.
Threads of our fate, drawn with care,
In every heartbeat, a spell in the air.

Through echoes of ages, our stories will weave,
In the book of the cosmos, together believe.
Ancient and bold, we reach for the skies,
Love's sacred symbols, the truth never lies.

Unseen Fonts of Affection

In the margins of life, our love becomes ink,
Unseen fonts of affection, more than you think.
Delicate strokes that touch and caress,
In quiet of whispers, our souls access.

Lines unbroken, yet hidden from view,
Each glance, each gesture, a story anew.
Ink spills softly, on pages unturned,
In the library of hearts, affection is learned.

Reflections in silence, where feelings collide,
A language unspoken, where hearts can confide.
In the quietest moments, our truths find their place,
Through unseen fonts, I cherish your grace.

In a world of noise, where chaos entwines,
Our written affection, like moonlight, defines.
Let the letters dance, in a rhythm so sweet,
In unseen fonts, our hearts find their beat.

Echoes in the Chamber

Within the chamber, echoes resound,
Whispers of memories, lost and found.
Walls hold the laughter, the shadows that loom,
Carving our stories, in dusk's gentle gloom.

Faded reflections, where time stands still,
Each echo a promise, a heart's silent thrill.
In the silence of moments, our feelings ignite,
Drawing us closer, in the soft twilight.

Chasing the shadows, we walk hand in hand,
Echoes of love, like grains of fine sand.
In the labyrinth of whispers, our spirits confined,
Every heartbeat a promise, forever entwined.

Let the echoes linger in this sacred space,
In the chamber of hearts, we find our embrace.
Resounding through ages, a heartbeat, a flame,
In echoes of love, we whisper our name.

Fables Written in Pulses

In shadows deep, secrets sing,
Whispers echo, hearts take wing.
Tales of old, in silence weave,
Promises held, in dreams we believe.

Beats entwined, like roots below,
Stories shared, in moonlight's glow.
Each pulse a tale, a breath bestowed,
Life's fables written, paths we rode.

The Manuscript of Hidden Affections

In margins inked, love's trace remains,
Softly penned, amidst life's strains.
Words unspoken, yet felt so near,
Lines of longing, in silence steer.

Pages turn, hearts lay bare,
In the quiet, we find each layer.
Written softly, in twilight's glow,
Hidden affections, in shadows flow.

The Unveiling of Inner Vaults

Behind closed doors, treasures hide,
Secrets murmur, emotions bide.
To unveil what lies beneath,
Is to dance in truth's own sheath.

Walls of steel, begin to crack,
With each word, there's no turning back.
Revealing layers, deep and raw,
Inner vaults, the heart's true draw.

The Tapestry of Unseen Connections

Threads of fate, woven tight,
Invisible bonds, pure delight.
In every glance, in every sigh,
The tapestry grows, reaching the sky.

Colors blend, and patterns form,
Bearing witness to love's warm.
In unseen threads, our spirits soar,
Connections thrive, forevermore.

Milton Keynes UK
Ingram Content Group UK Ltd.
UKHW021938121124
451129UK00007B/135